MY HEALTHY HABITS

KEEP CLEAN

TO KEEP HEALTHY

Norwood House Press

Madison Parker

Cataloging-in-Publication Data

Names: Parker, Madison.
Title: Keep clean to keep healthy / Madison Parker.
Description: Buffalo, NY : Norwood House Press, 2026. | Series: My healthy habits | Includes glossary and index.
Identifiers: ISBN 9781978575349 (pbk.) | ISBN 9781978575356 (library bound) | ISBN 9781978575363 (ebook)
Subjects: LCSH: Hygiene--Juvenile literature.
Classification: LCC RA780.P375 2026 | DDC 613--dc23

Published in 2026 by
Norwood House Press
2544 Clinton Street
Buffalo, NY 14224

Designer: Rhea Magaro
Editor: Kim Thompson

Photo credits: Cover, p. 1 JLco Julia Amaral/Shutterstock.com; p. 5 Ermolaev Alexander/Shutterstock.com; pp. 6,9,21 PeopleImages.com Yuri A/Shutterstock.com; p. 7 christinarosepix/Shutterstock.com; p. 8 johnfoto18/Shutterstock.com; p. 11 Magomed Magomedagaev/Shutterstock.com; p. 12 Lopolo/Shutterstock.com; p. 13 Veja/Shutterstock.com; p. 14 Kazitafahnizeer/Shutterstock.com; p. 15 myboys.me/Shutterstock.com; p. 17 Leestudio/Shutterstock.com; p. 18 Gregory Johnston/Shutterstock.com; p. 19 Trzykropy/Shutterstock.com

Printed in the United States of America

CPSIA compliance information: Batch #CSNHP26: For further information contact Norwood House Press at 1-800-237-9932.

TABLE OF CONTENTS

STAYING CLEAN IS IMPORTANT

Staying clean is an important way to keep your body healthy. Cleaning with soap and water washes away **germs** that can make you sick.

WASHING YOUR HANDS

Washing your hands with soap and water is one of the best **habits** for staying healthy. Remember to wash your hands before you eat, after you use the bathroom, and after you play outside.

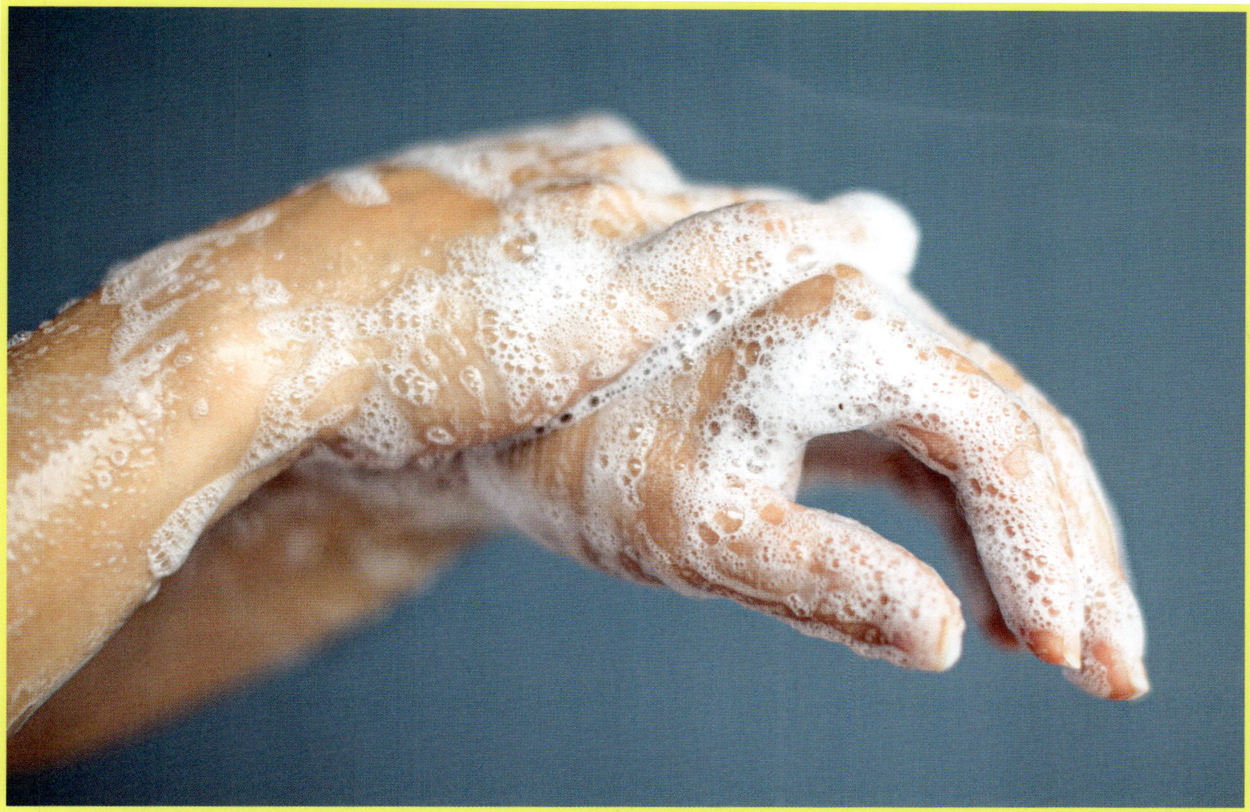

Scrub your hands for at least 20 seconds. That is about the amount of time it takes to sing “Happy Birthday” twice. Be sure to wash between your fingers and under your nails.

BRUSHING YOUR TEETH

Brush your teeth in the morning and at night. This removes bits of food and **plaque** that can cause **cavities**.

Brush for a **minimum** of two minutes. Make sure to clean the front, back, and top of each tooth. Brushing your tongue keeps it fresh.

BATHING AND SHOWERING

Taking a bath or shower keeps your body clean and healthy. It washes away dirt, sweat, and germs. Using soap and warm water removes oils and **bacteria** from your skin.

Washing your hair with shampoo removes dirt and oils from your **scalp**. It also makes your hair feel soft and smell nice.

After you bathe, dry your skin with a clean towel. Put on clean clothes to keep your body fresh.

CARING FOR YOUR HANDS AND FEET

Washing your hands and feet stops **odors**. After washing, apply lotion. This prevents dryness and keeps your skin soft.

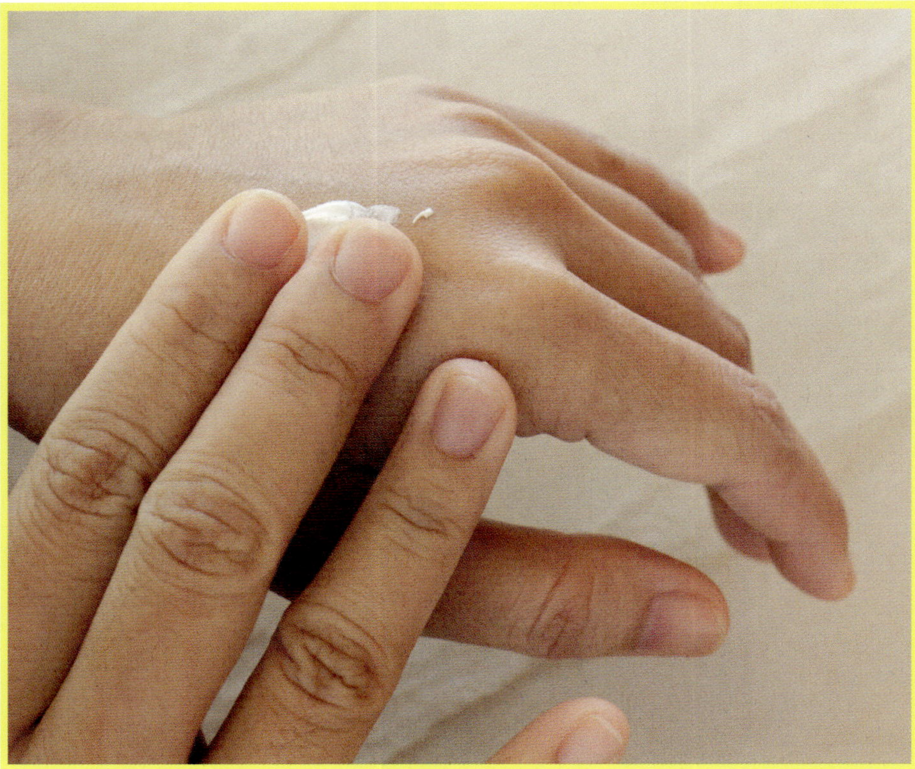

Wearing clean socks and well-fitting shoes protects your feet from blisters.

Keep your fingernails and toenails **trimmed** so they do not get too long. This will keep dirt and germs from collecting under them. Trim nails straight across so they do not grow into your skin.

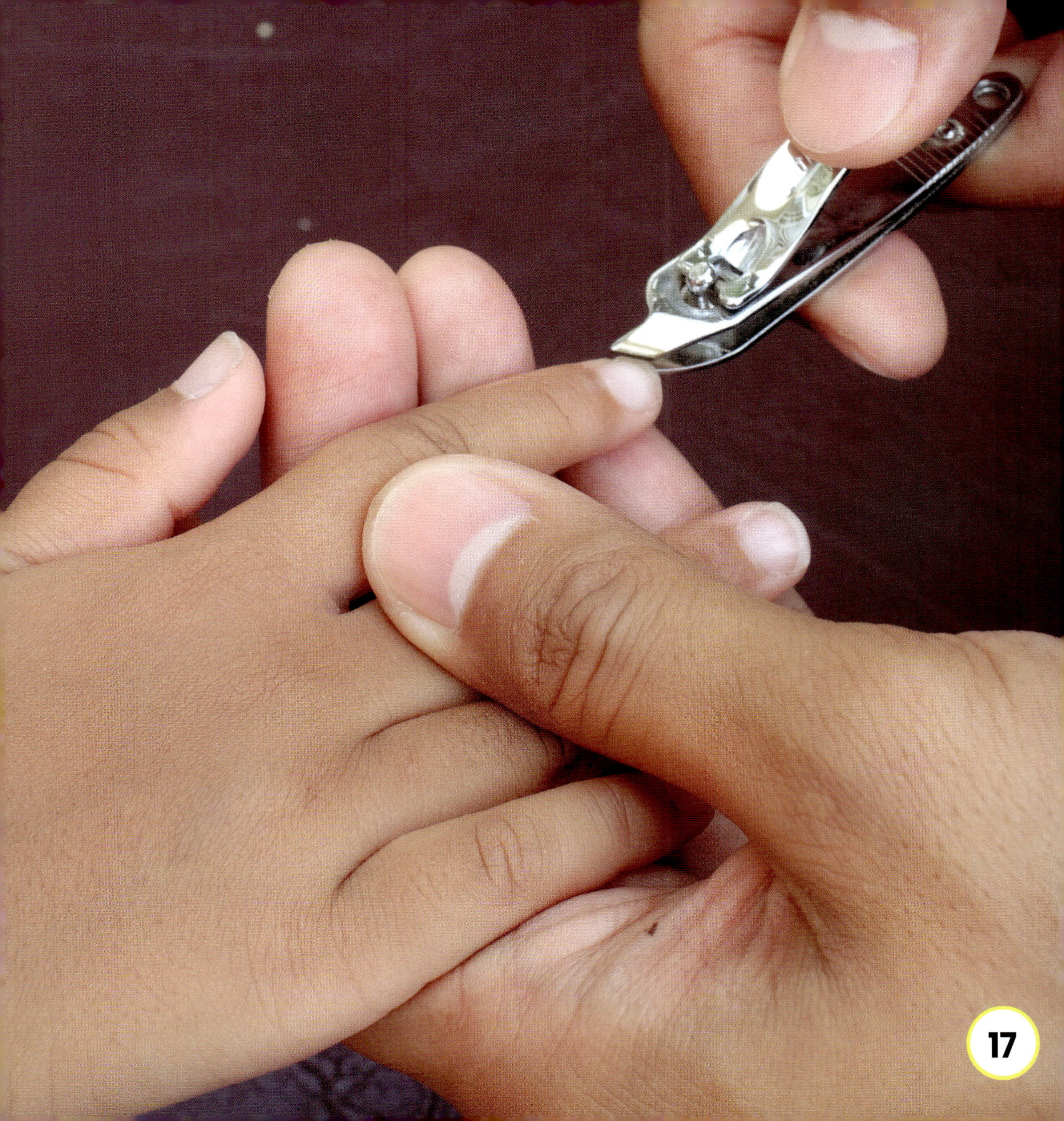

WEARING CLEAN CLOTHES

The clothes on your body collect dirt, sweat, and germs. Change into clean clothes after you get sweaty. This will prevent rashes and help keep your skin comfortable.

Fresh clothes smell nice and look tidy. Wearing clean socks and underwear every day is especially important for staying clean and preventing odors.

CLEAN AND HEALTHY

Washing your hands, taking care of your body, and wearing clean clothes are good habits. They help keep you healthy. They protect you from germs. Staying clean helps you feel your best every day!

GLOSSARY

bacteria (bak-TEER-ee-uh): tiny living things that can cause disease

cavities (KAV-i-teez): holes in the teeth caused by decay

germs (jurmz): tiny living things that can make you sick if they stay on or in your body

habits (HAB-itz): activities that you do on a regular basis

minimum (MIN-uh-muhm): the least or smallest amount you need to do

odors (OH-durz): smells, especially bad ones

plaque (plak): a sticky layer of germs that can build up on teeth and cause cavities

scalp (scalp): the skin on the top of your head that is usually covered by hair

scrub (skruhb): to rub something hard to make it clean

trimmed (trimd): cut to a shorter length

THINKING QUESTIONS

1. Why is it important to take baths or showers?
2. How does washing your hands stop germs from spreading?
3. For how long should you brush your teeth?
4. When should you put on clean clothes?
5. How does trimming your nails help keep you healthy?

INDEX

ABOUT THE AUTHOR

Madison Parker spent her childhood in the city of Chicago, Illinois. A farm girl at heart, today she lives in Wisconsin with her husband and four children on a small farm with cows, goats, chickens, and two miniature horses named Harley and David. Her favorite dessert is vanilla frozen custard with rainbow sprinkles, even in the winter.